My Reading Record

Name _____

D1509734

From _____ to _____

DAY PREP

DAY PREP

Reading Levels	Date	High Frequency Words
1 Kindergarten		
2		
3 Early First		
4		
5		
6		
7		
8		
9		
10 Mid First		
11		
12		
13		
14		
15		
16 Exit First		
17 Early Second		
18		
19		
20 Mid Second		
21		
22 Exit Second		
23 Early Third		
24		
25		
26 Exit Third		
27 Mid Fourth		
28 Exit Fourth		
29 Mid Fifth		
30 Exit Fifth		

_____ 6th   _____ 7th   _____ 8th   _____ 9th

_____ 10th   _____ 11th   _____ 12th

DAY PREP

Running Record   Date_____

Text_____ Level _____Comp_____

Errors_____ SC _____ Percent_____ Independent Instructional Frustrational		
	E	SC
Fluency _____ / Totals		

Running Record   Date_____

Text_____ Level _____Comp_____

Errors_____ SC _____ Percent_____ Independent Instructional Frustrational		
	E	SC
Fluency _____ / Totals		

DAY PREP

Running Record   Date_____

Text_____ Level _____Comp_____

Errors_____ SC _____ Percent_____	Independent	Instructional	Frustrational	
			E	SC
Fluency _____		/	Totals	

Running Record   Date_____

Text_____ Level _____Comp_____

Errors_____ SC _____ Percent_____	Independent	Instructional	Frustrational	
			E	SC
Fluency _____		/	Totals	

DAY PREP

Running Record   Date_____

Text_____ Level _____Comp_____

Errors_____ SC _____ Percent_____	Independent	Instructional	Frustrational		
				E	SC
Fluency _____		/	Totals		

Running Record   Date_____

Text_____ Level _____Comp_____

Errors_____ SC _____ Percent_____	Independent	Instructional	Frustrational		
				E	SC
Fluency _____		/	Totals		

DAY PREP

Running Record

Date_____

Text_____ Level _____ Comp_____

Errors_____ SC _____ Percent_____ Independent	Instructional	Frustrational		
			E	SC
Fluency _____	/	Totals		

Running Record

Date_____

Text_____ Level _____ Comp_____

Errors_____ SC _____ Percent_____ Independent	Instructional	Frustrational		
			E	SC
Fluency _____	/	Totals		

DAY PREP

Running Record   Date_____

Text_____ Level _____Comp_____

Errors_____ SC _____ Percent_____ Independent Instructional	Frustrational	
	E	SC
Fluency _____ / Totals		

Running Record   Date_____

Text_____ Level _____Comp_____

Errors_____ SC _____ Percent_____ Independent Instructional	Frustrational	
	E	SC
Fluency _____ / Totals		

DAY PREP

Running Record   Date_____

Text_____ Level _____Comp_____

Errors_____ SC _____ Percent_____ Independent Instructional Frustrational		
	E	SC
Fluency _____ / Totals		

Running Record   Date_____

Text_____ Level _____Comp_____

Errors_____ SC _____ Percent_____ Independent Instructional Frustrational		
	E	SC
Fluency _____ / Totals		

DAY PREP

Running Record   Date_____

Text_____ Level _____Comp_____

Errors_____ SC _____ Percent_____	Independent	Instructional	Frustrational		
				E	SC
Fluency _____		/	Totals		

Running Record   Date_____

Text_____ Level _____Comp_____

Errors_____ SC _____ Percent_____	Independent	Instructional	Frustrational		
				E	SC
Fluency _____		/	Totals		

DAY PREP

Running Record   Date_____

Text_____ Level _____Comp_____

Errors_____ SC _____ Percent_____ Independent	Instructional	Frustrational		
			E	SC
Fluency _____		/	Totals		

Running Record   Date_____

Text_____ Level _____Comp_____

Errors_____ SC _____ Percent_____ Independent	Instructional	Frustrational		
			E	SC
Fluency _____		/	Totals		

DAY PREP

Running Record   Date_____

Text_____ Level _____Comp_____

Errors_____ SC _____ Percent_____ Independent Instructional Frustrational	E	SC
Fluency _____ / Totals		

Running Record   Date_____

Text_____ Level _____Comp_____

Errors_____ SC _____ Percent_____ Independent Instructional Frustrational	E	SC
Fluency _____ / Totals		

DAY PREP

Running Record   Date_____

Text_____ Level _____ Comp_____

Errors_____ SC _____ Percent_____ Independent Instructional Frustrational		
	E	SC
Fluency _____ / Totals		

Running Record   Date_____

Text_____ Level _____ Comp_____

Errors_____ SC _____ Percent_____ Independent Instructional Frustrational		
	E	SC
Fluency _____ / Totals		

DAY PREP

Running Record

Date_____

Text_____ Level _____Comp_____

Errors_____ SC _____ Percent_____	Independent	Instructional	Frustrational		
				E	SC
Fluency _____		/	Totals		

Running Record

Date_____

Text_____ Level _____Comp_____

Errors_____ SC _____ Percent_____	Independent	Instructional	Frustrational		
				E	SC
Fluency _____		/	Totals		

DAY PREP

Running Record

Date_____

Text_____ Level _____ Comp_____

Errors_____ SC _____ Percent_____	Independent	Instructional	Frustrational	
			E	SC
Fluency _____	/	Totals		

Running Record

Date_____

Text_____ Level _____ Comp_____

Errors_____ SC _____ Percent_____	Independent	Instructional	Frustrational	
			E	SC
Fluency _____	/	Totals		

DAY PREP

Running Record   Date_____

Text_____ Level _____Comp_____

Errors_____ SC _____ Percent_____	Independent	Instructional	Frustrational		
				E	SC
Fluency _____		/	Totals		

Running Record   Date_____

Text_____ Level _____Comp_____

Errors_____ SC _____ Percent_____	Independent	Instructional	Frustrational		
				E	SC
Fluency _____		/	Totals		

DAY PREP

Running Record   Date_____

Text_____ Level _____Comp_____

Errors_____ SC _____ Percent_____ Independent Instructional Frustrational		
	E	SC
Fluency _____ / Totals		

Running Record   Date_____

Text_____ Level _____Comp_____

Errors_____ SC _____ Percent_____ Independent Instructional Frustrational		
	E	SC
Fluency _____ / Totals		

DAY PREP

Running Record   Date_____

Text_____ Level _____Comp_____

Errors_____ SC _____ Percent_____ Independent Instructional Frustrational	E	SC
Fluency _____ / Totals		

Running Record   Date_____

Text_____ Level _____Comp_____

Errors_____ SC _____ Percent_____ Independent Instructional Frustrational	E	SC
Fluency _____ / Totals		

DAY PREP

Running Record

Date_____

Text_____ Level _____ Comp_____

Errors_____ SC _____ Percent_____ Independent Instructional Frustrational		
	E	SC
Fluency _____ / Totals		

Running Record

Date_____

Text_____ Level _____ Comp_____

Errors_____ SC _____ Percent_____ Independent Instructional Frustrational		
	E	SC
Fluency _____ / Totals		

DAY PREP

Running Record   Date_____

Text_____ Level _____Comp_____

Errors_____ SC _____ Percent_____	Independent	Instructional	Frustrational		
				E	SC
Fluency _____		/	Totals		

Running Record   Date_____

Text_____ Level _____Comp_____

Errors_____ SC _____ Percent_____	Independent	Instructional	Frustrational		
				E	SC
Fluency _____		/	Totals		

DAY PREP

Running Record   Date_____

Text_____ Level _____ Comp_____

Errors_____ SC _____ Percent_____ Independent Instructional Frustrational		
	E	SC
Fluency _____ / Totals		

Running Record   Date_____

Text_____ Level _____ Comp_____

Errors_____ SC _____ Percent_____ Independent Instructional Frustrational		
	E	SC
Fluency _____ / Totals		

DAY PREP

Running Record   Date_____

Text_____ Level _____Comp_____

Errors_____ SC _____ Percent_____	Independent	Instructional	Frustrational		
				E	SC
Fluency _____		/	Totals		

Running Record   Date_____

Text_____ Level _____Comp_____

Errors_____ SC _____ Percent_____	Independent	Instructional	Frustrational		
				E	SC
Fluency _____		/	Totals		

DAY PREP

Running Record   Date_____

Text_____ Level _____ Comp_____

Errors_____ SC _____ Percent_____ Independent Instructional Frustrational	E	SC
Fluency _____ / Totals		

Running Record   Date_____

Text_____ Level _____ Comp_____

Errors_____ SC _____ Percent_____ Independent Instructional Frustrational	E	SC
Fluency _____ / Totals		

DAY PREP

Running Record   Date_____

Text_____ Level _____Comp_____

Errors_____ SC _____ Percent_____ Independent Instructional Frustrational	E	SC
Fluency _____ / Totals		

Running Record   Date_____

Text_____ Level _____Comp_____

Errors_____ SC _____ Percent_____ Independent Instructional Frustrational	E	SC
Fluency _____ / Totals		

DAY PREP

Running Record   Date_____

Text_____ Level _____Comp_____

Errors_____ SC _____ Percent_____	Independent	Instructional	Frustrational		
				E	SC
Fluency _____		/	Totals		

Running Record   Date_____

Text_____ Level _____Comp_____

Errors_____ SC _____ Percent_____	Independent	Instructional	Frustrational		
				E	SC
Fluency _____		/	Totals		

DAY PREP

Running Record   Date_____

Text_____ Level _____Comp_____

Errors_____ SC _____ Percent_____ Independent Instructional Frustrational		
	E	SC
Fluency _____ / Totals		

Running Record   Date_____

Text_____ Level _____Comp_____

Errors_____ SC _____ Percent_____ Independent Instructional Frustrational		
	E	SC
Fluency _____ / Totals		

DAY PREP

Running Record   Date_____

Text_____ Level _____Comp_____

Errors_____ SC _____ Percent_____ Independent Instructional	Frustrational	
	E	SC
Fluency _____ / Totals		

Running Record   Date_____

Text_____ Level _____Comp_____

Errors_____ SC _____ Percent_____ Independent Instructional	Frustrational	
	E	SC
Fluency _____ / Totals		

DAY PREP

Running Record   Date_____

Text_____ Level _____Comp_____

Errors_____ SC _____ Percent_____ Independent Instructional Frustrational		
	E	SC
Fluency _____ / Totals		

Running Record   Date_____

Text_____ Level _____Comp_____

Errors_____ SC _____ Percent_____ Independent Instructional Frustrational		
	E	SC
Fluency _____ / Totals		

DAY PREP

Running Record   Date_____

Text_____ Level _____ Comp_____

Errors_____ SC _____ Percent_____ Independent Instructional Frustrational		
	E	SC
Fluency _____ / Totals		

Running Record   Date_____

Text_____ Level _____ Comp_____

Errors_____ SC _____ Percent_____ Independent Instructional Frustrational		
	E	SC
Fluency _____ / Totals		

DAY PREP

Running Record

Date_____

Text_____ Level _____Comp_____

Errors_____ SC _____ Percent_____ Independent Instructional Frustrational	E	SC
Fluency _____ / Totals		

Running Record

Date_____

Text_____ Level _____Comp_____

Errors_____ SC _____ Percent_____ Independent Instructional Frustrational	E	SC
Fluency _____ / Totals		

DAY PREP

Running Record   Date_____

Text_____ Level _____Comp_____

Errors_____ SC _____ Percent_____ Independent	Instructional	Frustrational		
			E	SC
Fluency _____	/	Totals		

Running Record   Date_____

Text_____ Level _____Comp_____

Errors_____ SC _____ Percent_____ Independent	Instructional	Frustrational		
			E	SC
Fluency _____	/	Totals		

DAY PREP

Running Record   Date_____

Text_____ Level _____Comp_____

Errors_____ SC _____ Percent_____ Independent Instructional	Frustrational	
	E	SC
Fluency _____ / Totals		

Running Record   Date_____

Text_____ Level _____Comp_____

Errors_____ SC _____ Percent_____ Independent Instructional	Frustrational	
	E	SC
Fluency _____ / Totals		

DAY PREP

Running Record   Date_____

Text_____ Level _____ Comp_____

Errors_____ SC _____ Percent_____ Independent Instructional Frustrational		
	E	SC
Fluency _____ / Totals		

Running Record   Date_____

Text_____ Level _____ Comp_____

Errors_____ SC _____ Percent_____ Independent Instructional Frustrational		
	E	SC
Fluency _____ / Totals		

DAY PREP

Running Record   Date_____

Text_____ Level _____Comp_____

Errors_____ SC _____ Percent_____ Independent Instructional	Frustrational	
	E	SC
Fluency _____ / Totals		

Running Record   Date_____

Text_____ Level _____Comp_____

Errors_____ SC _____ Percent_____ Independent Instructional	Frustrational	
	E	SC
Fluency _____ / Totals		

DAY PREP

Running Record   Date_____

Text_____ Level _____Comp_____

Errors_____ SC _____ Percent_____	Independent	Instructional	Frustrational		
				E	SC
Fluency _____		/	Totals		

Running Record   Date_____

Text_____ Level _____Comp_____

Errors_____ SC _____ Percent_____	Independent	Instructional	Frustrational		
				E	SC
Fluency _____		/	Totals		

DAY PREP

Running Record   Date_____

Text_____ Level _____Comp_____

Errors_____ SC _____ Percent_____ Independent Instructional	Frustrational	
	E	SC
Fluency _____ / Totals		

Running Record   Date_____

Text_____ Level _____Comp_____

Errors_____ SC _____ Percent_____ Independent Instructional	Frustrational	
	E	SC
Fluency _____ / Totals		

DAY PREP

Running Record   Date_____

Text_____ Level _____Comp_____

Errors_____ SC _____ Percent_____ Independent Instructional Frustrational		
	E	SC
Fluency _____ / Totals		

Running Record   Date_____

Text_____ Level _____Comp_____

Errors_____ SC _____ Percent_____ Independent Instructional Frustrational		
	E	SC
Fluency _____ / Totals		

DAY PREP

Running Record

Running Record   Date_____

Text_____ Level _____ Comp_____

Errors_____ SC _____ Percent_____	Independent	Instructional	Frustrational		
				E	SC
Fluency _____			/	Totals		

Running Record   Date_____

Text_____ Level _____ Comp_____

Errors_____ SC _____ Percent_____	Independent	Instructional	Frustrational		
				E	SC
Fluency _____			/	Totals		

DAY PREP

Running Record   Date_____

Text_____ Level _____Comp_____

Errors_____ SC _____ Percent_____ Independent Instructional Frustrational		
	E	SC
Fluency _____ / Totals		

Running Record   Date_____

Text_____ Level _____Comp_____

Errors_____ SC _____ Percent_____ Independent Instructional Frustrational		
	E	SC
Fluency _____ / Totals		

DAY PREP

Running Record   Date_____

Text_____ Level _____Comp_____

Errors_____ SC _____ Percent_____ Independent Instructional	Frustrational	
	E	SC
Fluency _____ / Totals		

Running Record   Date_____

Text_____ Level _____Comp_____

Errors_____ SC _____ Percent_____ Independent Instructional	Frustrational	
	E	SC
Fluency _____ / Totals		

DAY PREP

Running Record

Date_____

Text_____ Level _____Comp_____

Errors_____ SC _____ Percent_____	Independent	Instructional	Frustrational	
			E	SC
Fluency _____	/	Totals		

Running Record

Date_____

Text_____ Level _____Comp_____

Errors_____ SC _____ Percent_____	Independent	Instructional	Frustrational	
			E	SC
Fluency _____	/	Totals		

DAY PREP

Running Record   Date_____

Text_____ Level _____Comp_____

Errors_____ SC _____ Percent_____	Independent	Instructional	Frustrational	E	SC
Fluency _____		/	Totals		

Running Record   Date_____

Text_____ Level _____Comp_____

Errors_____ SC _____ Percent_____	Independent	Instructional	Frustrational	E	SC
Fluency _____		/	Totals		

DAY PREP

Running Record   Date_____

Text_____ Level _____Comp_____

Errors_____ SC _____ Percent_____ Independent Instructional	Frustrational	
	E	SC
Fluency _____ / Totals		

Running Record   Date_____

Text_____ Level _____Comp_____

Errors_____ SC _____ Percent_____ Independent Instructional	Frustrational	
	E	SC
Fluency _____ / Totals		

DAY PREP

Running Record   Date_____

Text_____ Level _____Comp_____

Errors_____ SC _____ Percent_____ Independent Instructional Frustrational	E	SC
Fluency _____ / Totals		

Running Record   Date_____

Text_____ Level _____Comp_____

Errors_____ SC _____ Percent_____ Independent Instructional Frustrational	E	SC
Fluency _____ / Totals		

At one magical moment in your early childhood, the page of a book--that string of confused, alien ciphers--shivered into meaning. Words spoke to you, gave up their secrets; at that moment, whole universes opened. You became, irrevocably, a reader.

--Albert Manguel, A History of Reading

DAY PREP

Made in the USA
Middletown, DE
15 February 2022